Mt. Diablo Wildflowers

Mount Diablo Wildflowers
© Copyright 2005
by Mt. Diablo Interpretive Association
All rights Reserved
P. O. Box 346
Walnut Creek, CA 94597-0346

ISBN 0-9748925-0-5

CONTENTS

ACKNOWLEDGEMENTS

In Memory of Betty Goldstein

Text by Bill Pierson, Linda Sanford

Photographs by Amy Erez, Tom Harris, Michael O'Brien, Dave M. Peck, Bill Pierson, and Yulon Tong

Design and Illustrations by Tom Camara
Cover photograph: Bill Pierson

Edited by Mary Beth Keller, Jackie Pierson, Linda Sanford, and Yulon Tong

MT. DIABLO WILDFLOWERS

An isolated peak in the middle of California, Mt. Diablo has its own unique flora. Over time, this has resulted in a diverse mixture of plants, some of which are found only on Mt. Diablo. Many plants have their southern or northern-most limits here.

The aim of this guide is to give the reader a tool for use in identifying some of the more showy wildflowers on the mountain. To make the guide easy to use, it is first divided into the following color groups: White, Yellow/Orange, Red/Pink, and Blue/Violet. Plant family then categorizes each color group.

Accompanying each photograph is a brief description of the flower, giving details of location, identification and/or cultural information. Look at the flower diagrams and mini-glossary of terms in the back of the guide for more clarification.

Please note that much of the information in this guide comes from a previous MDIA wildflower brochure and other great sources on plants. For those who would like to learn more about Mt. Diablo's flora, refer to the bibliography at the end of the guide. These books will give the reader more in-depth information about the amazing flora of Mt. Diablo.

Yulon Tong

SOAP ROOT or WAVY LEAF
(Chlorogalum pomeridianum)

Lily Family
(Liliaceae)

Herb

Blooms: May - Jul

Soap, thread, and food are a few of the ways this plant was used by California Indians. On hot spring and summer nights, soap plants can be seen blooming in many locations in grasslands and open woodlands.

Bill Pierson

MARIPOSA LILY
(Calochortus venustus)

Lily Family
(Liliaceae)

Herb

Blooms: May - Jul

The petals of the mariposas, Spanish for butterfly, have exquisite varicolored spots, lines and splotches. Look for mariposas in the upper part of Donner Canyon, Mitchell Canyon and around Rock City.

Bill Pierson

FREMONT STAR LILY
(Zigadenus fremontii)

Lily Family
(Liliaceae)

Herb

Blooms: Mar - Apr

One of our early chaparral treasures, the Fremont star lily shoots up glossy green leaves followed by dense spires of creamy star like flowers. Colonies proliferate especially after fire has stricken an area. Common in open woodlands and chaparral areas.

Bill Pierson

POISON OAK
(Toxicodendron diversiloba)

Sumac Family
(Anacardiaceae)

Shrub, Vine

Blooms: Apr

Yes, it has flowers! After the leaves turn red the flowers are equally toxic. Poison oak is found throughout the mountain. "Leaflets three, let it be" is a fitting motto for this plant.

Bill Pierson

POISON HEMLOCK
(Conium maculatum)

Carrot Family
(Apiaceae)

Herb

Blooms: Jun - Jul

Note the umbrella or umbel of flowers and the lacy leaves. Purple spots on the stems are also indicative of this species. This non-native has been confused with elderberry with deadly results. It can be found in low-lying areas of Mitchell Canyon.

Bill Pierson

NARROW LEAF MILKWEED
(Asclepias fascicularis)

Milkweed Family
(Asclepiadiaceae)

Herb

Blooms: Jun - Jul

If you see a green oasis in a sea of dry grasses, you may be seeing the narrow leaf milkweed. Watch out for Monarch butterflies circling these flowers in the heat of summer, especially off Red Road. One of two milkweeds on the mountain, narrow leaf milkweed can be found throughout the mountain at elevations from 300 to 2800 feet.

Bill Pierson

YARROW
(Achillea millefolium)

Sunflower Family
(Asteraceae)

Herb

Blooms: Apr - Jun

Yarrow is a circumboreal species, a species that is found worldwide. Note the fern-like leaves. It has been used for medicinal purposes, including lowering fevers, and can be found in grassy areas at all elevations on the mountain.

Bill Pierson

CALIFORNIA EVERLASTING
(Gnaphalium californicum)

Sunflower Family
(Asteraceae)

Herb

Blooms: Jun - Jul

Also called cudweed. During the dry summer months this everlasting smells like sweet maple syrup. Everlastings can be found throughout the mountain, especially along the road to the summit.

Bill Pierson

WILD RADISH
(Raphanus sativa)

Mustard Family
(Brassicaceae)

Herb

Blooms: Apr - Jun

This European non-native is common through-out California in a variety of habitats. On Mt. Diablo it can be found in disturbed areas along North Gate Road heading towards the summit.

Yulon Tong

MILK MAIDS
(Cardamine californica)

Mustard Family
(Brassicaceae)

Herb

Blooms: Jan - Apr

These showy white flowers are often the first flow-ers to come out on the mountain. Look for long or pinnate leaflets of 3 below singular 4-petal flow-ers. Milk maids can be found from 1000 feet to the summit in a variety of habitats including open chaparral, the summit and in wooded canyons.

DOUGLAS SANDWORT
(Minuartia douglasii)

Pink Family
(Caryophyllaceae)

Herb

Blooms: Apr - May

This low-growing plant is found in dry, shallow soils on rocky slopes in Donner Canyon and on Eagle Ridge and Deer Ridge.

MORNING GLORY
(Calystegia sp.)

Morning Glory Family
(Convolvulaceae)

Vine

Blooms: Apr

This plant is a vine with cone-shaped flowers. Morning glories can be found trailing along the ground, along the sides of many trails in Donner Canyon, Mitchell Canyon and near Pine Creek.

Tom Harris/Bill Pierson

WILD CUCUMBER
(Marah fabaceus)

Cucumber Family
(Cucurbitaceae)

Vine

Blooms: Apr

Also called manroot from the large, often man-sized roots hidden under ground. This vine is frequently found trailing over bushes and up trees. The fruit is not edible, but can be dried and the spines removed to make a scrubbing sponge. Found throughout the mountain, especially in woodlands.

Bill Pierson

MANZANITA
(Arctostaphylos sp.)

Heath Family
(Ericaceae)

Shrub

Blooms: Dec - Mar

Spanish for "little apples," manzanita is known for its smooth red bark, stiff leaves, urn-shaped flowers and clusters of apple-like fruits. Mt. Diablo Manzanita (*Artostaphylos auriculata*) is endemic to Mt. Diablo. Manzanitas occur in chaparral areas throughout the mountain.

Bill Pierson

CALIFORNIA BUCKEYE
(Aesculus californica)

Buckeye Family
(Hippocastanaceae)

Tree

Blooms: May - Jun

Candles of white flowers appear in late spring and early summer. The fruit, a little larger than a golf ball, was used by California Indians to stupefy fish in creeks and streams. Buckeye graces canyon bottoms throughout the foothills.

Bill Pierson

WHITE NEMOPHILIA
(Nemophila heterophila)

Waterleaf Family
(Hydrophyllaceae)

Herb

Blooms: Mar - Apr

Found from 400 feet to the summit throughout the mountain, white nemophila is most common in shady woodlands. This picture was taken in the shade of oak trees at Mitchell Canyon.

Bill Pierson

YERBA SANTA
(Eriodictyon californicum)

Waterleaf Family
(Hydrophyllaceae)

Shrub

Blooms: May - Jun

Also called Indian chewing gum, the leaves have a shiny dark upper side and a woolly gray underside. Yerba santa, meaning "holy shrub" in Spanish, is found in many chaparral areas. Butterflies eagerly feed upon the nectar of these flowers, especially along the Globe Lily Trail in Mitchell Canyon.

Bill Pierson

PITCHER SAGE
(Lepichinia calycima)

Mint Family
(Lamiaceae)

Shrub

Blooms: May - Jun

The inflated sepals resemble upside-down pitchers. Leaves have a quilt-like texture and have a strong smell. Pitcher sage can be found from 1000 feet to the summit. Mitchell Canyon and the road to the summit are good places to look.

Bill Pierson

BLACK SAGE
(Salvia mellifera)

Mint Family
(Lamiaceae)

Shrub

Blooms: Apr - Jul

Blooming in hot chaparral areas, black sage is a tall shrub that attracts a multitude of insects in the summer. Found near the yerba santas on the chaparral portion of the Globe Lily Trail at Mitchell Canyon.

Michael O'Brien

TREE ANEMONE
(Carpenteria californica)

Mock Orange Family
(Philadelphaceae)

Tree

Blooms: May - Aug

A transplant, probably from Fresno County, this shrub was planted near Donner Cabin along with other non-natives including daffodils and fuchsia-flowered gooseberry.

Bill Pierson

MINER'S LETTUCE
(Claytonia perfoliata)

Purslane Family
(Portulacaceae)

Herb

Blooms: Feb - May

California gold rush miners used the succulent leaves of this plant as a preventative against scurvy. Found in many oak woodland areas.

Yulon Tong

BITTER ROOT
(Lewisia rediviva)

Purslane Family
(Portulacaceae)

Herb

Blooms: Apr - Jun

The scientific name originates from Meriwether Lewis of the Lewis & Clark expedition of 1804. Lewisia is also the state flower of Montana. Found at higher elevations on the mountain, especially in rocky scree.

Bill Pierson

VIRGIN'S BOWER
(Clematis ligustifolia)

Buttercup Family
(Ranunculaceae)

Vine

Blooms: Jul - Aug

Found at lower elevations of Mitchell Canyon, this rare species of Virgin's bower grows on areas of northern exposure. The blooms of this woody vine are as impressive as the fruit that follows.

Bill Pierson

BUCK BRUSH
(Ceanothus cuneatus)

Buckthorn Family
(Rhamnaceae)

Shrub

Blooms: Feb - Apr

A shrub commonly associated with chaparral throughout the Mt. Diablo foothills. The miniature petals are spatulate in shape. This picture was taken at the Fire Interpretive Trail.

CHAMISE
(Adenostoma fasciculatum)

Rose Family
(Rosaceae)

Shrub

Blooms: Jun

Chamise is our most abundant chaparral shrub, covering hundreds of acres. In early June, shrubs are covered in a froth of thousands of tiny white flowers.

CALIFORNIA BLACKBERRY
(Rubus ursinus)

Rose Family
(Rosaceae)

Vine

Blooms: Apr

Leaflets of three are commonly mistaken for poison oak, but blackberry leaves are hairy and prickly. Blackberries are commonly found near the creeks that flow through many canyons.

TOYON
(Heteremoles arbutifolia)

Rose Family
(Rosaceae)

Shrub

Blooms: Jun - Jul

Also known as California Holly, this plant is a tough, long-lived chaparral shrub noted for its handsome leaves and large clusters of red holly-like berries. Toyon occurs in chaparral and open woodlands.

CALIFORNIA ROSE
(Rosa californica)

Rose Family
(Rosaceae)

Shrub

Blooms: May - Jun

Commonly found along the margins of creek beds and near fencerows, the flower petals range in color from creamy white to pink. The fruit, commonly called "hips" is high in Vitamin C.

Bill Pierson

BEDSTRAW
(Gallium sp.)

Madder Family
(Rubiaceae)

Vine

Blooms: Apr - Jun

Also called goosegrass or cleavers, bedstraw is found in shady areas at all elevations. Bedstraw was purportedly used as a stuffing material for early pioneers. It is often seen in association with miner's lettuce.

Yulon Tong

CALIFORNIA SAXIFRAGE
(Saxifraga californica)

Saxifrage Family
(Saxifragaceae)

Herb

Blooms: Feb - Apr

Note the whorl of leaves at the base of the stem. This is a feature that identifies many members of the saxifrage family. Look in shady wooded areas throughout the mountain at elevations from 800 to 3500 feet.

WOODLAND STAR
(Lithophragma sp.)

Saxifrage Family
(Saxifragaceae)

Herb

Blooms: Mar - Apr

We have three species of *Lithophragma* on the mountain. Look for white flowers with snowflake-like petals arising out of long stems and leaves whorled at the bottom of the plant. Woodland Stars are common in open woodlands.

BELLARDIA
(Bellardia trixago)

Figwort Family
(Scrophulariaceae)

Herb

Blooms: Apr - May

A non-native species from Europe, Bellardia is a widespread annual frequently found in grasslands and disturbed places.

Bill Pierson

YELLOW MARIPOSA LILY
(Calochortus luteus)

Lily Family
(Liliaceae)

Herb

Blooms: May - Jun

Tiny beetles are important pollinators of this flower. Look deep within the corolla or flower petals. Like the other mariposas, this flower is found in open grassy areas.

Bill Pierson

MT. DIABLO GLOBE TULIP
(Calochortus pulchellus)

Lily Family
(Liliaceae)

Herb

Blooms: May - Jun

This variety of globe tulip is only found on Mt. Diablo. In woodlands, it lights up shaded nooks in late spring. It is found in many areas of the mountain. Look for good displays in Mitchell Canyon and along Stage Road near Castle Rock.

CHECKER LILY
(Fritillaria affinis (lanceolata))

Lily Family
(Liliaceae)

Herb (bulb)

Blooms: Mar
- May

Look for stalks carrying several lovely hanging bells, checkered and mottled in unusual colors. Checker lilies are frequently found in lightly-shaded areas on the northern side of the mountain. The above pictures were taken in Mitchell Canyon off Globe Lily Trail and in Donner Canyon on the way to the Falls Trail.

BLOW-WIVES
(Achyrachaena mollis)

Sunflower Family
(Asteraceae)

Herb

Blooms: Apr

The fruits of this sunflower relative (shown above) are showier than the diminutive yellow flowers. The wind picks up these pretty fruits and "blows" them away. Look for them in the grasslands between Donner and Mitchell Canyons.

Bill Pierson

YELLOW STAR THISTLE
(Centaurea solstitialis)

Sunflower Family
(Asteraceae)

Invasive Shrub

Blooms: Jul - Oct

This non-native from southern Europe is considered a pest plant. Yellow star thistles have been known to take over large areas of grassland and crowd out native species. It is especially prevalent along the sides of roads and other disturbed areas.

Bill Pierson

GOLDENBUSH
(Ericameria linearifolia)

Sunflower Family
(Asteraceae)

Shrub

Blooms: Apr - Jun

One of our two species of *Ericameria* - look for a dark green bush covered with yellow daisies. In midspring, the narrow sticky leaves carry it through summer heat and drought. Goldenbush can be seen on the hillsides when traveling through Mitchell Canyon.

Yulon Tong

OREGON SUNSHINE or WOOLLY SUNFLOWER
(Eriophyllum lanatum)

Sunflower Family
(Asteraceae)

Herb

Blooms: May - Jun

These small yellow flowers are found in rocky, exposed areas from 400 feet to the summit. Check Donner Canyon, Mitchell Canyon and the south side of the Fire Interpretive Trail.

Bill Pierson

GUMWEED
(Grindelia camporum)

Sunflower Family
(Asteraceae)

Herb

Blooms: May - Oct

This long blooming flower is found on open grassy edges and hillsides. Found in many areas. Check Fossil Ridge or Pine Canyon.

Bill Pierson

MT. DIABLO SUNFLOWER
(Helianthella castanea)

Sunflower Family
(Asteraceae)

Herb

Blooms: Apr

Restricted to the Mt. Diablo area, this sunflower carries bright yellow daisies inches above the foliage. It favors open brushy places. This picture was taken from off the side of summit road between Toyon and Roundtop picnic areas.

Glen Keater

GOLDFIELDS
(Lasthenia californica)

Sunflower Family
(Asteraceae)

Herb

Blooms: Mar - Apr

These miniature yellow daisies literally carpet rolling open grasslands by the thousands in spring. Only inches tall, they make up for size in their numbers.

Bill Pierson

MULE'S EARS
(Wyethia glabra)

Sunflower Family
(Asteraceae)

Herb

Blooms: Apr

We have three species of mule's ears on the mountain. If you find broad floppy leaves that resemble real mule's ears, you may have found this flower. Large yellow sunflower-like blossoms show their relationship to daisies. Look for them on steep slopes throughout the mountain.

Bill Pierson

FIDDLENECK
(Amsinckia menziesii var. intermedia)

Borage Family
(Boraginaceae)

Herb

Blooms: Mar - Apr

Named for the flower buds coiled into the fiddle-neck shape of a violin. As the coil unwinds, the flower opens. Note the dark spots inside the small orange flowers. To find fiddlenecks, look in open grassy areas throughout the mountain from the base to 2800 feet.

Bill Pierson

WESTERN WALLFLOWER
(Erysimum capitatum)

Mustard Family
(Brassicaceae)

Herb

Blooms: Mar - May

The large yellow flowers of this wallflower are especially prolific at Devil's Elbow and along the Fire Interpretive Trail near the summit. Note the four-petal flowers, a hallmark of the mustard family.

Bill Pierson

BLUE ELDERBERRY
(Sambucus mexicana)

Sheep Sorrel Family
(Caprifoliaceae)

Shrub

Blooms: Mar - Jun

Often found near roadsides and streams. The botanical name Sambucus is derived from a Greek musical instrument made from elderwood. Common in canyons.

ROCK LETTUCE
(Dudleya cymosa)

Stonecrop Family
(Crassulaceae)

Herb

Blooms: May - Jun

A succulent with small yellow flowers that is found hugging the rocks on talus slopes from Mitchell Canyon upward to the summit.

DEER WEED
(Lotus scoparius)

Pea Family
(Fabaceae)

Herb/Shrub

Blooms: May - Jul

A small yellow and red flowered perennial found in disturbed areas. It is a pioneer species that fertilizes or adds nitrogen to the soil with the help of symbiotic bacteria. Found at the margins of chaparral.

Bill Pierson

CALIFORNIA BAY LAUREL
(Umbellularia californica)

Laurel Family
(Lauraceae)

Tree

Blooms: Dec - Feb

Smell the bay scented evergreen leaves and view the nectar-rich saucer-like yellow blossoms. Bay trees favor moist north-facing slopes or canyon bottoms.

Bill Pierson

COMMON BROOMRAPE
(Orobanche fasciculata)

Broomrape Family
(Orobanchaceae)

Herb

Blooms: Mar - Apr

Like other species in the broomrape family, this plant is a root parasite of chaparral plants such as chamise. Common broomrape can be found along Red Road off of Mitchell Canyon during the early spring months.

Bill Pierson

GOLDEN EARDROPS
(Dicentra chrysantha)

Poppy Family *(Papaveraceae)*

Herb

Blooms: Apr

This plant is common only after fire. It has soaring flowering stalks with upturned bright yellow bleeding heart-like shaped flowers. Occasional plants crop up on rocky slopes near the summit. This photograph was taken Toyon picnic area.

Glen Keater

CREAM CUPS
(Platystemon californicus)

Poppy Family *(Papaveraceae)*

Herb

Blooms: Feb - Mar

A delicate poppy relative with nodding buds and shallow saucer like cream-colored flowers, often marked with spots of yellow. Good stands can be expected in many grassy areas after generous winter rains.

Dave M. Peck

CALIFORNIA POPPY
(Eschscholzia californica)

Poppy Family
(Papaveraceae)

Herb

Blooms: Apr - Jun

Our state flower, the California poppy is also one of our most beautiful with lustrous satiny orange petals and multiple orange stamens. Poppies illuminate many rolling grasslands throughout the foothills.

Michael O'Brien

WIND POPPY
(Stylomecon heterophylla)

Poppy Family
(Papaveraceae)

Herb

Blooms: Apr - Jun

The crumpled dark orange petals of the wind poppy lie almost flat, unlike the cup-shaped blossoms of California poppy. Search for this fragile wildflower in the rocky areas of Mitchell Canyon and Donner Canyon.

Bill Pierson

SULFUR BUCKWHEAT
(Eriogonumum umbellatum)

Buckwheat Family
(Polygonaceae)

Herb

Blooms: Jun

This spindly plant is immediately recognized by the sulfur-hued blossoms and circular clumps of small pale green leaves that hug the ground. Look for it on rocky shelves near the summit.

Bill Pierson

CALIFORNIA BUTTERCUP
(Ranunculus californicus)

Buttercup Family
(Ranunculaceae)

Herb

Blooms: Feb - Mar

One of our earliest wildflowers, California buttercup bears shellacked yellow blossoms just as oaks start to leaf. Fine displays grace open woodlands on the Coulter Pine Trail and throughout the foothills.

Bill Pierson

BUSH MONKEY-FLOWER
(Mimulus aurantiacus)

Figwort or Penstemon Family *(Scrophulariaceae)*

Shrub

Blooms: Mar - Jun

The bush monkeyflower is a small shrub with sticky leaves. It is transformed in late spring and summer by the orange two-lipped flower that suggests faces. Look for it along the margins of chaparral throughout the mountain.

Bill Pierson

GOLDEN MONKEYFLOWER
(Mimulus guttatus)

Figwort or Penstemon Family *(Scrophulariaceae)*

Shrub

Blooms: Apr - Jun

Blossoms of the golden monkeyflower mimic animal faces with two lips and throat. The lower lip is freckled with brownish spots. Look for it on seeps along North Gate Road or by the stream in Pine Canyon.

Bill Pierson

WILD PANSY
(Viola pedunculata)

Family
(Violaceae)

Herb

Blooms: Apr - May

A yellow violet with distinct petals, wild pansy has flowers that may never open. Look for its pansy faces in company with buttercups along the Coulter Pine Trail.

Yulon Tong

SICKLE-LEAVED ONION
(Allium falcifolium)

Lily Family
(Liliaceae)

Herb

Blooms: Apr - Jun

Found in open rocky areas at elevations above 2300 feet, sickle-leaved onion has flat, and curved leaves. The summit and North Peak are good places to look.

Yulon Tong

SERRATED ONION
(Allium serra)

Lily Family
(Liliaceae)

Herb

Blooms: Apr - May

Found in woody areas from the base of Mt. Diablo to 3000 feet. Good places to search include Mitchell Canyon and Donner Canyon.

Bill Pierson

**COLONIAL
ONION**
*(Allium
unifolium)*

Lily Family
(Liliaceae)

Herb

Blooms: Apr - Jun

Note the singular leaf or "unifolium" and the star shaped flowers. This onion is often found in shady woodland locations.

Bill Pierson

**GIANT
TRILLIUM**
*(Trillium
chloropetalum)*

Lily Family
(Liliaceae)

Herb

Blooms: Mar
- May

A splendid forest dweller, giant trillium has three large, often mottled leaves. In the middle sits a single maroon, white or green flower. Count yourself lucky to find this trillium. Best bet: Sycamore Canyon.

COBWEB THISTLE
(Cirsium occidentale)

Sunflower Family
(Asteraceae)

Herb

Blooms: May - Jun

Cobwebby hairs, tall slender stems and dense heads of tubular red or lavender flowers identify this native. Cobweb thistle is seen near the summit and along the Fire Interpretive Trail.

BREWER'S ROCKCREST
(Arabis breweri)

Mustard Family
(Brassicaceae)

Herb

Blooms: Mar - Apr

Look for small pale green leaves and beautiful pink to purple flowers on rocky outcrops from 100 feet to the summit. Brewer's rockcrest can also be identified by its curved seedpods that arise after flowering. The summit area is the best site to study this species, but also look for it at the Falls Trail in Donner Canyon.

Yulon Tong

CALIFORNIA HONEY-SUCKLE
(Lonicera hispidula)

Honeysuckle Family
(Caprifoliaceae)

Shrub

Blooms: May - Jun

We have two honeysuckles on the mountain. Pairs of leaves join at the stem. This variety is found in shady areas, especially near streams. It is found at elevations of 500 to 2200 feet.

Bill Pierson

CHAPARRAL PEA
(Pickeringia Montana)

Pea Family
(Fabaceae)

Shrub

Blooms: May

Note the pea-like flowers that light up this dark green leaved shrub. Found in the chaparral areas of Curry Canyon, Donner Canyon and Emmons Canyon.

Yulon Tong

CHAPARRAL CURRANT
(Ribes malvaceum)

Gooseberry or
Currant Family
(Grossulariaceae)

Shrub

Blooms: Jan - Mar

Light pink to pale purple flower trusses hang below sticky leaves from late fall to early spring. Bluish berries follow. This currant is common in chaparral and open woodlands.

Yulon Tong

CANYON GOOSEBERRY
(Ribes menziesii)

Gooseberry or
Currant Family
(Grossulariaceae)

Shrub

Blooms: Apr - Jun

Note the dense clusters of prickly spines. This gooseberry carries tiny nodding red and white fuchsia-like flowers under its leafy stems. You'll find canyon gooseberry in many wooded habitats.

Bill Pierson

FREMONT BUSH MALLOW
(Malacothamnus fremontii)

Hibiscus Family
(Malvaceae)

Shrub

Blooms: Jun - Oct

Common only after fire, the Fremont bush mallow can be identified by its white felted leaves and cup-shaped flowers. Look in chaparral areas such as Lime Ridge or upper Mitchell Canyon.

Bill Pierson

HUMMINGBIRD FUCHSIA
(Epilobium canum)

Evening Primrose Family
(Onagraceae)

Herb

Blooms: Aug - Nov

It goes unnoticed until late summer, when the flared scarlet trumpets lure hummingbirds and humans alike. This fuchsia favors rocky shelves or gravely slopes throughout the mountain.

Bill Pierson

**RED RIBBONS
CLARKIA**
*(Clarkia
concinna)*

Evening Primrose
Family
(Onagraceae)

Herb

Blooms: May - Jun

Note the three lobed petals on this variety. Red ribbons clarkia covers mossy banks with its electric pink flowers, trimmed in red. You'll find red ribbons under dense shrubberies on the Fire Interpretive Trail in Mitchell Canyon. Clarkias were named to honor William Clark of the Lewis and Clark expedition.

Michael O'Brian

**ELEGANT
CLARKIA**
*(Clarkia
unguiculata)*

Evening Primrose
Family
(Onagraceae)

Herb

Blooms: Apr - Jun

Found throughout Mitchell Canyon, elegant clarkia, along with other members of the evening primrose family has 4 petals and exhibits ovaries that occur well below the flower on the stem.

Bill Pierson

WINECUP CLARKIA
(Clarkia purpurea ssp. viminea)

Evening Primrose Family
(Onagraceae)

Herb

Blooms: May - Jun

In contrast to red ribbons, winecup clarkia has small cup-shaped, wine-colored blossoms atop tall stalks. On the inside of the petals are dark red blotches. Search for winecup clarkias along the Summit Road and in grassy areas throughout the mountain.

Bill Pierson

CLAYTONIA
(Claytonia gypsophiloides)

Purslane Family
(Portulacaceae)

Herb

Blooms: Apr - May

A small, bright pink flower that occurs on steep rocky slopes at high elevations. Check the Fire Interpretive Trail on the summit, Deer Ridge, North Peak and Mt. Olympia.

Yulon Tong

RED MAIDS/ BREWERS CALANDRINIA
(Calandrinia ciliata and C. breweri)

Purslane Family
(Portulacaceae)

Herb

Blooms: Jan - May

Our two species of Calandrinia have small red flowers and are found in disturbed areas. Brewer's calandrinia is frequently found in chaparral areas and blooms from March to May. Red maids are found on grassy slopes.

Michael O'Brien

COLUMBINE
(Aquilegia sp.)

Buttercup Family
(Ranunculaceae)

Herb

Blooms: May (Woodland Columbine)
Jun - Jul (Stream Columbine)

Columbines are found in moist areas, especially along shaded streamsides. We have two varieties on the mountain. This one was found in Donner Canyon.

Bill Pierson

SCARLET LARKSPUR
(Delphinium nudicaule)

Buttercup Family
(Ranunculaceae)

Herb

Blooms: Mar - Jun

This flower is unusual for its flame color as most larkspurs have blue or purple flowers. Note how the upper sepal tapers back into a slender, nectar holding spur. Look for scarlet larkspur in open rocky areas throughout the mountain, especially at higher elevations.

Michael O'Brien

INDIAN PAINT-BRUSHES
(Castilleja spp.)

Penstemon Family
(Scrophularia-ceae)

Herb (parasite)

Blooms: Mar - Jun

Perhaps one of our most long-lasting chaparral flowers, Indian paintbrushes can be recognized by their vivid orange or red flower spikes. The color comes from floral bracts and sepals, not petals. Paintbrushes are conspicuous on slopes along the edges of woodlands and chaparral.

Bill Pierson

INDIAN WARRIOR
(Pedicularis densiflorus)

Penstemon Family
(Scrophulariaceae)

Herb (parasite)

Blooms: Feb - May

Note the deep red bracts blossoming just above its coarsely divided, fernlike leaves. You'll often find Indian warrior in close association with manzanitas. Dan Cook Canyon and the Falls Trail above Donner Canyon are good places to look.

Yulon Tong

RED ROCK PENSTEMMON
(Keckiella corymbosa)

Penstemon Family
(Scrophularia-ceae)

Herb

Blooms: Jul - Sep

Sprouting out of rocky outcrops, red rock penstemon is one of the late arriving flowers on Mt. Diablo. Look for this drought-tolerant performer near the summit.

Bill Pierson

RED MONKEY FLOWER
(Mimulus cardinalis)

Penstemon Family *(Scrophularia-ceae)*

Herb

Blooms: Aug - Oct

This striking monkeyflower is found in stream-beds next to the water's edge in places such as Mitchell Canyon and in Donner Canyon.

Bill Pierson

CALIFORNIA FIGWORT
(Scrophularia californica)

Penstemon Family *(Scrophularia-ceae)*

Herb

Blooms: Apr - Jun

Found in shady areas, often leaning on nearby shrubs, this tiny flower is wonderful to behold close up. Note how the leaves are arranged opposite each other. Found at altitudes from 400 feet to the summit. Also called Bee Plant because it is favored by bees.

Yulon Tong

SHORT SPURRED PLECTRITIS
(Plectritis macrocera)

Valerian Family
(Valerianaceae)

Herb

Blooms: Mar - May

This annual is found from 1000 feet to the summit on slopes that are grassy or rocky. Check Mitchell Canyon, Deer Flat and North Peak.

Bill Pierson

ITHURIEL'S SPEAR
(Triteleia laxa)

Lily Family
(Liliaceae)

Herb

Blooms: Apr - May

Note the trumpet shaped flowers in open flower arrangements. Ithuriel's spear flowers in mid-spring, well after blue dicks have finished. Look for Ithuriel's spear in grassy woodlands.

Bill Pierson

BLUE DICKS
(Dichelostemma sp.)

Lily Family
(Liliaceae)

Herb

Blooms: Mar - May

Often referred to as brodiaea. Note the congested arrangement of small pale blue to purplish flowers and two sets of a series of three anthers inside the flower. Blue dicks is common in grassy areas.

GREATER PERIWINKLE
(Vinca major)

Dogbane Family
(Apocynaceae)

Vine

Blooms: Mar - Apr

This weed from Europe is considered a pest in riparian areas because it crowds out native species. Commonly used as an ornamental, Vinca may come from the Latin "to conquer." It can be found in Mitchell Canyon below 1000 feet.

PURPLE SALSIFY
(Tragopogon porrifolius)

Sunflower Family
(Asteraceae)

Herb

Blooms: May

Not only are the flowers of this annual beautiful to behold, but also the fruit looks like a large dandelion. Look for this European exotic along the first part of the trail leading upwards in Mitchell Canyon and in Pine Canyon near Pine Pond.

Tom Harris

HOUND'S TONGUE
(Cynoglossum grande)

Borage Family
(Boraginaceae)

Herb

Blooms: Feb - Mar

Hound's tongue is a harbinger of spring. The elegant blue flowers resemble those of forget-me-nots, right down to the central rim. Found from 750 feet to the summit on the north side of the mountain. Look in Rhine Canyon, Donner Canyon, Mitchell Canyon and Deer Flat.

Bill Pierson

SILVER LUPINE
(Lupinus albifrons)

Pea Family
(Fabaceae)

Herb/Shrub

Blooms: Mar - May

Silver lupine is our largest lupine and takes the form of an herbaceous shrub. You will find it along with other lupines in grasslands and along the edges of oak woodlands. Note the many-fingered leaves and pea-like flowers.

Bill Pierson

BABY BLUE EYES
(Nemophila menziesii)

Waterleaf Family
(Hydrophyllaceae)

Herb

Blooms: Mar - Apr

Baby blue eyes sprawls low to the ground while soils are still moist. Each blue blossom shows a contrasting central white patch. Fine stands of baby blue eyes occur around Deer Flat and in Donner Canyon.

Yulon Tong

TANSY-LEAF PHACELIA
(Phacelia tanacetifolia)

Waterleaf Family
(Hydrophyllaceae)

Herb

Blooms: Apr - May

Known to cover entire slopes in good years, the tansy-like fern-like leaves and long protruding purple stamens identify it. Search in Mitchell and Back Canyons.

BLUE-EYED GRASS
(Sisyrinchium bellum)

Iris Family
(Iridaceae)

Herb

Blooms: Mar - Apr

Look for slender iris-like leaves and shallow saucer-shaped blue-purple petals striped with dark purple and yellow centers. Blue-eyed grass is common in grasslands.

COYOTE MINT
(Monardella villosa)

Mint Family
(Lamiaceae)

Herb

Blooms: Jun - Jul

Coyote mint has strong sage-like scented leaves. Flowers bloom in the heat of summer. Common in Back Canyon, Dan Cook Canyon, and along Fossil Ridge, Lime Ridge, and Shell Ridge.

Yulon Tong

VINEGAR WEED
(Trichostema lanceolatum)

Mint Family
(Lamiaceae)

Herb

Blooms: Aug - Sep

Found in hot grassy fields, vinegar weed has stems and leaves that have a sticky residue that smells like vinegar. Common in the Black Hills, on Lime Ridge, and along Oyster Point Road.

Yulon Tong

BIRD'S EYE GILIA
(Gilia tricolor)

Phlox Family
(Polemoniaceae)

Herb

Blooms: Mar - Apr

Each pale blue flower is centered in dark purple, with a yellow throat and complemented by blue pollen. You'll find drifts of bird's eye gilia at Deer Flat or along the Waterfall Trail.

Tom Harris

SHOOTING STAR
(Dodecatheon hendersonii)

Primrose Family
(Primulaceae)

Herb

Blooms: Mar - Apr

An early bloomer, shooting star flowers have pink or purple petals and projecting beak-like stamens. Shooting stars grace moist hillsides with northerly exposures in Donner Canyon, Mitchell Canyon, Dan Cook Canyon and at Deer Flat.

Bill Pierson

ROYAL LARKSPUR
(Delphinium variegatum)

Buttercup Family
(Ranunculaceae)

Herb

Blooms: Apr - Jun

One of our five blue delphiniums on the mountain, royal larkspur is found in shady oak woodlands or on grassy slopes. Look for it at Coulter Pine Trail, Rock City or Fossil Ridge.

Bill Pierson

PURPLE OWL'S CLOVER
(Castilleja exserta)

Penstemon Family
(Scrophulariaceae)

Herb

Blooms: Mar - May

Purple owl's clover is not a clover at all and is related to paintbrushes. Like them, the color comes from floral bracts that look as though someone has dipped them in pink paint. You'll see them near Deer Flat and Devil's Elbow as well as along Burma Road and Pine Creek.

Bill Pierson

CHINESE HOUSES
(Collinsia heterophylla)

Penstemon Family
(Scrophulariaceae)

Herb

Blooms: Apr - Jun

Note the two-toned flowers arranged in elegant whorls. It graces oak woodlands, from the upper reaches of Mitchell Canyon, Donner Canyon, Pine Canyon, and Sycamore Canyon to the summit.

Bill Pierson

FEW-FLOWERED COLLINSIA
(Collinsia sparsiflora)

Penstemon Family *(Scrophularia-ceae)*

Herb

Blooms: Mar - May

A relative of Chinese houses, this very small collinsia is found in very rocky areas on the summit and in Donner and Mitchell Canyons in moist woody areas.

Yulon Tong

VARICOLORED PENSTEMON
(Penstemon heterophyllus)

Penstemon Family *(Scrophularia-ceae)*

Herb

Blooms: Apr - May, Jun

Violet bushes of the varicolored penstemon are found above 2100 feet on the rocky hillsides next to the road to the summit.

Tom Harris

BLUE WITCH
(Solanum umbelliferum)

Tomato Family
(Solanaceae)

Shrub

Blooms: Mar - May

Blue witch is a small, green-twigged bush transformed by hundreds of saucer-shaped blue flowers. Flowers have a yellow center with small green dots on cup shaped blue petals. Look for it in Mitchell Canyon or on the Fire Interpretive Trail along the fringes of chaparral.

Generalized Flower Diagram

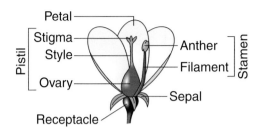

Petal
Stigma
Style
Pistil
Ovary
Receptacle
Anther
Filament
Stamen
Sepal

Ovary Placement

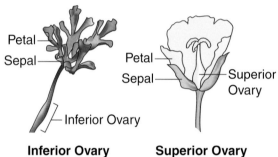

Petal
Sepal
Inferior Ovary

Petal
Sepal
Superior Ovary

Inferior Ovary
(Red Ribbons Clarkia)

Superior Ovary
(Yellow Mariposa Lily)

Leaf Arrangement

Whorled   **Opposite**   **Alternate**

MINI-GLOSSARY

Anther: Where pollen is produced.

Bract: A petal or leaf like appendage encircling a flower.

Chaparral: Dry areas with dense groupings of drought tolerant shrubs.

Filament: A stem-like support for the anther.

Fruit: A ripened ovary. Once a flower becomes pollinated fruit may be formed.

Ovary: Where ovules are produced that eventually may turn into seeds upon fertilization of the flower. See flower diagrams for superior and inferior ovary placement.

Receptacle: A bulbous area below the sepals of a flower.

Pistil: The female part of the plant that consists of the stigma, style, ovary and ovaries. This is where seeds are produced.

Sepal: A layer of petal like structures that are frequently green and surround an inner layer of petals.

Stamen: Consists of the anther and filament and is the male portion of the flower – where pollen in produced.

Scree: Loose rock or gravel on the side of a steep slope.

Seed: Ripened ovule.

Stigma: Where pollen first enters the pistil.

Style: A tube through which pollen travels to fertilize ovules that later may become seeds. The style is located between the stigma and ovary.

Talus: A sloping mass of rock fragments at the base of a cliff.

RECOMMENDED READING

1. ERTTER, B. and BOWERMAN, M.L. 2002. *The Flowering Plants and Ferns of Mt. Diablo,* CA. California Native Plant Society. An un-illustrated book that describes the flora of Mt. Diablo and where to find individual species. The geology of Mt. Diablo is also discussed in some detail.

2. BEIDLEMAN, L.H. and KOZLOFF, E.N. 2003. *Plants of the San Francisco Bay Region, Mendocino to Monterey.* University of California Press. This book has photographs of most of the major wildflowers that are found in northern Calif.

3. KEATER, G., 1994. *Plants of the East Bay Parks.* Mt. Diablo Interpretive Association. This book is out of print, but is worth finding for the great keys, illustrations and narrative.

4. NIEHAUS, T.F, and RIPPER, C.L. 1976. *Pacific State Wildflowers.* Houghton Mifflin. Fully illustrated, but a little out of date, this book is an excellent tool for learning how to key wildflowers.

5. HICKMAN, J.C. 1993. *The Jepson Manual.* University of California Press. A fully illustrated plant bible for the serious and amateur botanist. Almost all (if not all) native plants in California are covered in this masterpiece.

COMMON NAME INDEX

COMMON NAME INDEX

COMMON NAME INDEX

COMMON NAME INDEX

FLOWER NOTES